# RECOGNIZE THE CADENCE - THE NARCISSIST'S OFFENSIVE PLAYBOOK

# RECOGNIZE THE CADENCE - THE NARCISSIST'S OFFENSIVE PLAYBOOK

TINA R PAONE

TALL OAKS
PUBLISHING

Recognize the Cadence: The Narcissist's Offensive Playbook

By Dr. Tina R. Paone
Edited by Jennifer S. Gabriel
Acknowledgments to Alex Romagnoli

Published by Tall Oaks Publishing
Lansdale, PA
ISBN: 979-8-9944043-2-4
Printed in the United States of America
First Edition

# CONTENTS

# Disclaimer and Safety Notice

The information provided in this Book is for informational and educational purposes only. It is not intended to be a substitute for professional mental health counseling, medical advice, or legal services. The content within this book should not be used to diagnose or treat any condition.

This playbook uses football terminology strictly as a metaphor to describe patterns of psychological manipulation and emotional abuse. It is not intended to reference, stereotype, or disparage football players, coaches, teams, or the sport itself. Football is used solely as a familiar strategic language to help clarify complex relational dynamics. The behaviors described are not inherent to athletics or football culture, and the intent is education—not judgment.

## Immediate Safety Warning

If you are in immediate danger, fear for your safety, or are in an emergency situation, please stop reading and contact your local emergency services (such as 911), a trusted support system, or a domestic violence hotline immediately (800-799-7233 or text "BEGIN" to 88788.)

## Personal Responsibility

Every individual's situation is unique and potentially high-risk. You must assess your own circumstances and safety before enacting any suggestions or strategies mentioned in this book. The author and publisher assume no responsibility for any actions taken or consequences resulting from the application of the information provided herein.

## Safety Planning

The suggestions in this book are most effective when integrated into a comprehensive, personalized safety plan. We strongly encourage you to work with a trained advocate or professional to develop a plan that addresses your specific needs and environment.

# How to Read this Playbook

Being in a narcissistic relationship often feels like playing a game with a rigged rule-book—one where the rules change mid-play, violations are ignored, and you're blamed for outcomes you never controlled. Over time, that confusion can make you doubt your instincts, your memory, and even your sense of self.

This playbook was written to help you see the game clearly. Its purpose is not to label people or diagnose motives, but to identify patterns—the repeatable plays narcissists use to gain control, protect their image, and keep you reacting instead of living. Chaos feels personal. But when you can identify the patterns within the chaos, it becomes recognizable.

Each play in this book follows the same structure so you can learn to spot these tactics as they happen, not just in hindsight. You do not need to read this book in order. Go directly to the play that matches what you're experiencing right now. Recognition alone can be grounding. It restores language, validates what you've felt, and confirms a critical truth: what you experienced was real.

This playbook focuses on awareness. It helps you name what's happening on the field so confusion loses its power. Once you can recognize the cadence, you are no longer playing blind. The next step—learning how to respond, protect yourself, and reclaim your footing—is explored in the companion volume, *The Invincible Defense: Counter to the Narcissist's Playbook.*

# Teams

Every game has two sides. In narcissistic systems, understanding who is on the field—and what role they play—helps explain why the same dynamics repeat, even when you change your behavior.

### The Offensive Unit (The Narcissistic System)

In a narcissistic abuse system, the Offensive Unit is designed to advance power, avoid accountability, and keep control of the game.

**The Narcissist is the Quarterback (QB).** This is the central decision-maker who controls the ball and calls every play. They decide who is targeted, how the play unfolds, and when to pivot, all while demanding loyalty and obedience.

**The Primary Victim is the Ball.** The goal is not partnership but possession. The Ball does not choose where it goes; it is moved, controlled, passed, or sacrificed to advance the play. Every action on the field revolves around controlling the Ball. (Note: This metaphor reflects the narcissist's mindset—not your worth, agency, or humanity.)

**Blocking Backs / Fullbacks represent Enablers, also known as "Flying Monkeys".** Their job is to clear the path for the Quarterback, ignoring challenges, absorbing impact, and protecting the play. Many are unaware they're playing this role, believing they're "helping," "keeping the peace," or that the Quarterback narrative is reality.

**Offensive Linemen (Center, Guards, Tackles) represent Structural Enablers, also known as an Emotional Shield.** They form the wall directly in front of the Quarterback, absorbing pressure and preventing defenders (truth, accountability, consequences) from getting through. These can be family systems, workplace hierarchies, legal structures, or social norms that protect the narcissist by design, not intent.

**Wide Receivers and Tight Ends represent Distraction Enablers.** They run decoy routes—spreading misinformation, shifting focus, or creating side conflicts—to pull attention away from the abuse itself. Their role is confusion, misdirection, and plausible deniability, often without realizing they are part of the play.

Together, the Offensive Unit ensures one outcome: the Quarterback stays protected, the Ball stays controlled, and accountability never reaches the backfield.

## The Defensive Unit (Reality and Truth)

If the Offensive Unit exists to protect control, the Defensive Unit exists to restore reality. This is the opposition: the side of the field committed to truth, safety, and long-term healing.

**The Head Coach represents Therapists and Counselors.** As master strategists, they teach the defensive player how the opponent actually operates by breaking down the Narcissist's Playbook (the abuse cycle). They call timeouts through scheduled sessions and intentional rest, helping regulate the nervous system and prevent burnout. Their ultimate goal isn't to win a single play—it's to prepare the player for the decisive play: the Interception, often experienced as No Contact or firm, enforced boundaries.

**The Defensive Coordinator represents a Trusted Support Network.** These are the family and friends who hold reality steady. They provide grounding between drives, reinforce what actually happened, and restore morale when the Victim has been benched through devaluation or self-doubt. Their role is not strategy but stabilization: reminding the defender of their worth, strength, and sanity when the noise gets loud.

**The Film Analyst represents Education and Research.** This is the process of studying game tape—learning about narcissistic abuse, trauma bonding, gaslighting, and coercive control. By reviewing past plays, patterns become visible. The chaos stops feeling personal and starts looking predictable. Knowledge doesn't stop the offense, but it removes the element of surprise—and that changes the entire game.

Together, the Defensive Unit does what the offense cannot tolerate: it names reality, slows the game down, and makes escape not just possible, but sustainable.

# Object of the Game (And What Winning Really Means)

**For the Narcissist**

The object of the game is control. The narcissist's goal is to move, manipulate, or attack the Victim in order to dominate energy, attention, and freedom. Winning is not about scoring points or resolving conflict—it's about successfully executing the play and advancing their agenda.

A "win" occurs when the narcissist maintains power over the victim's emotions, reality, or focus.

**Win Condition #1: Gaining Supply and Control**

This is the ultimate victory. The narcissist successfully provokes an emotional reaction—anger, fear, guilt, sadness—and reinforces control over the victim's reality. Their narrative crosses the goal line, and the victim is pulled back into the system.

**Win Condition #2: Causing Emotional Damage**

This is a tactical win. Even if full control isn't achieved, the play succeeds by draining energy, creating self-doubt, or forcing the victim into reactive mode. As long as the victim is defending themselves instead of living freely, the drive continues.

**Win Condition #3: Isolating the Victim**

Here, the narcissist slowly corrodes the victim's relationships with others, creating an environment in which their support network is weakened. An ally is discredited and connections are discouraged.

**Win Condition #4: Maintaining the Game**

This is the long game. The narcissist keeps the abusive cycle active by keeping the victim engaged, confused, hopeful, or exhausted—focused on the narcissist instead of seeking clarity, help, or exit.

**For the Defense (The Victim)**

The defense does not win by scoring against the narcissist. It wins by ending the play.

Winning means recognizing patterns, naming reality, and refusing to keep advancing the narcissist's drive. Every time you see the play forming, enforce a boundary, disengage, or reclaim your attention, you stop the offense from gaining yards.

Throwing the challenge flag—even internally, through awareness—interrupts the game. Healing, clarity, and support build a defense so solid that the narcissist's plays stop working. The ultimate defensive win is not dominance; it's freedom.

# How This Playbook Is Structured

Each play in this book follows the same structure, giving you a consistent way to recognize narcissistic tactics, understand what's happening, and reclaim your footing.

### Play Title

This names the specific narcissistic tactic being used. Naming the pattern matters because confusion thrives in silence. When you can identify the play, you can respond with awareness instead of self-doubt.

### Football Play Name

This is a simple football analogy that illustrates how the tactic works. You don't need to understand football to understand the play: the analogy exists to make patterns easier to recognize, remember, and recall under stress.

### On-Field Analogy

This section walks through how the tactic unfolds in real life, step by step, often beginning subtly and escalating over time. Narcissistic abuse rarely looks abusive at first. This breakdown helps you see the setup, the shift, and the moment control is gained.

### Snaps (What You'll Hear or See)

These are common phrases, statements, or behaviors used during the play. Hearing the language and seeing the behaviors helps you recognize the tactic in real time and trust your instincts when something feels "off."

### Penalty

This is a clear, plain-language explanation of what's happening psychologically and emotionally. It grounds the play in reality—without minimizing the harm or overcomplicating the explanation—so the behavior can be understood and named for what it is.

### Role of the Offensive Unit (If Used)

Some plays rely on an Offensive Unit made up of Blockers, also known as enablers. Abuse rarely happens in isolation. Depending on the play, the narcissist may call Blockers in—or run the play alone—but the outcome is the same: accountability is deflected, and the victim is made to feel isolated or unreasonable.

Blockers may be people, such as "flying monkeys" deployed to distract, discredit, or apply pressure. They may also be systems or structures—family dynamics, workplace cultures, or social norms that prioritize image, loyalty, or hierarchy over truth. Blockers can even be internalized beliefs that train you to doubt yourself, stay quiet, or take the blame. Whether human or structural, their function is identical: protecting the narcissist and destabilizing the victim.

### Challenge Flag

This section names the emotional, psychological, or practical cost of the play to you. It centers impact rather than intent, identifying harm so it can no longer be minimized or dismissed. The challenge flag gives you the information needed to question what you're hearing or seeing—without questioning your sanity.

As you move through this playbook, remember: your goal is not to throw the challenge flag on every play or "win" every conversation. The object is learning to recognize the play, stop giving up easy yards, and reclaim your time, energy, and identity. A strong defense isn't reactive—it makes old tricks ineffective.

For strategies on how to respond, see *The Invincible Defense: Counter to the Narcissist's Playbook.*

# Play #1 - Love Bombing

### Football Play Name

The Touchdown on Opening Drive

### On-Field Analogy

The Quarterback launches a long, high-risk pass designed to cover massive ground fast. It's a move used when an immediate score is the priority. The goal is to overwhelm the defense before it has time to read the play, adjust coverage, or set boundaries.

### Snaps (What You'll Hear or See)

"I've never met anyone as perfect as you."

"You are my soulmate, I feel like I've known you forever."

"I want to spend every second of the day with you."

"I know we've only been dating for a couple of weeks, but I wanted you to have this (insert expensive gift/trip)."

"Everyone else in my life is so boring compared to you."

### Penalty

Love bombing floods a new victim with excessive attention, flattery, gifts, and grand gestures to create rapid attachment. The intensity feels intoxicating, but the bond is shallow and conditional—built for control, not connection.

### Role of the Offensive Unit (If Used)

Blockers stand ready to celebrate the catch and normalize the speed and intensity of the connection. They validate the narrative that "this is special," discouraging pause, reflection, or outside perspective.

### Challenge Flag

Intensity without time. Affection used to hook you before trust, safety, or reality can develop.

# Play #2 - Gaslighting

### Football Play Name
The Reverse Play

### On-Field Analogy
The Quarterback hands off the ball, but the running back suddenly reverses direction. What was clear a moment ago becomes disorienting, causing the defense to hesitate and doubt their read of the play.

### Snaps (What You'll Hear or See)
"You're imagining things—that never happened."
"You're too sensitive; you always overreact."
"I never said that; your memory is terrible."
"You need to stop being so paranoid."
"Are you sure? You always get things mixed up."

### Penalty
Gaslighting distorts reality by denying or twisting facts, slowly eroding your trust in your own memory, perception, and judgment.

### Role of the Offensive Unit (If Used)
Blockers reinforce the reversal, insisting the play went the opposite direction and that the defender is confused or unreliable.

### Challenge Flag
Reality distortion. When you start questioning what you clearly saw, felt, or remembered, you've already thrown the flag.

# Play #3 - Hoovering

### Football Play Name

The Draw Play

### On-Field Analogy

The Quarterback fakes a pass, drawing the defense forward, then hands the ball off for a run—regaining ground after boundaries were set.

### Snaps (What You'll Hear or See)

"I can't live without you—I've changed, I promise."
"I was so depressed after you left; I need you to help me."
"Let's just talk about the good times we had."
"I heard you're doing well; I just wanted to apologize for everything."
"It was my fault. I'll make everything right this time."

### Penalty

Hoovering is an attempt to "suck you back in" once you've pulled away. It mimics remorse or vulnerability to trigger guilt, hope, or responsibility—reopening the door so the cycle can restart.

### Role of the Offensive Unit (If Used)

Blockers briefly stop blocking, only to re-engage aggressively when the Narcissist runs back into the relationship.

### Challenge Flag

False remorse designed to pull you back in.

# Play #4 - Projection

### Football Play Name

Throwing the Ball into the Stands

### On-Field Analogy

The Quarterback frantically throws the ball to avoid an impending sack.

### Snaps (What You'll Hear or See)

"You're the one who is always lying to me."

"Why are you being so selfish all the time?"

"You're just projecting your insecurities onto me."

"I think you have an anger problem, not me."

"You are so controlling—you never let me do anything."

### Penalty

Projection shifts the narcissist's own traits or behaviors onto you, forcing you to defend against accusations that belong to them.

### Role of the Offensive Unit (If Used)

Blockers insist the Quarterback never had the ball and claim the victim started with it.

### Challenge Flag

Attributing their own flaws to you.

# Play #5 - Blame Shifting

### Football Play Name
The "Botched Handoff"

### On-Field Analogy
The Quarterback fumbles the exchange, creating the problem, then immediately turns and blames the running back for "poor ball security." The mistake is real, but responsibility is instantly redirected.

### Snaps (What You'll Hear or See)
"If you hadn't done that, I wouldn't have reacted this way."
"It's your fault I was late because you took too long to get ready."
"You pushed me to say those things."
"I wouldn't have had to lie if you were more understanding."
"This whole situation is because of your incompetence."

### Penalty
Blame shifting avoids accountability by assigning responsibility for the narcissist's actions to someone else—most often the victim.

### Role of the Offensive Unit (If Used)
Blockers reinforce the narrative that the mistake wasn't the Quarterback's fault, echoing claims of "poor ball security".

### Challenge Flag
Refusal to take responsibility.

# Play #6 - Triangulation

### Football Play Name
The Decoy Route

### On-Field Analogy
The Quarterback sends an additional player on a highly visible route, drawing the defense's attention away from the real play. While the defender focuses on the decoy, the Quarterback maintains control elsewhere.

### Snaps (What You'll Hear or See)
"My ex was so much better at supporting my career."
"Our mutual friend agrees with me that you are overreacting."
"Why can't you be more like (person's name)?"
"I have so many people who would love to be with me."
"You should hear what (person's name) says about how amazing I am."

### Penalty
Triangulation introduces a third party—real or implied—to create insecurity, competition, or validation, shifting power back to the narcissist.

### Role of the Offensive Unit (If Used)
Blockers amplify the decoy, steering attention toward the third party while reinforcing the narcissist's central position.

### Challenge Flag
Using others to control you.

# Play #7 - Silent Treatment

### Football Play Name

The Punt

### On-Field Analogy

The Quarterback cannot successfully complete the drive, handing over possession. The punt puts the defense on the 1-yard line. The play isn't about progress—it's about emotional distance and punishment.

### Snaps (What You'll Hear or See)

(Silence after being asked a question)
(Walking away mid-sentence)
(Ignoring texts or calls for days)
"I have nothing to say to you until you realize your mistake."
(Stonewalling and staring blankly)

### Penalty

The silent treatment withholds communication to punish, destabilize, and provoke anxiety, keeping the victim off-balance and focused on regaining connection.

### Role of the Offensive Unit (If Used)

Blockers isolate the victim by preventing outside support and reinforcing withdrawal as justified.

### Challenge Flag

Withdrawal as control.

# Play #8 - Devaluation

### Football Play Name

The Bench Warmer

### On-Field Analogy

The Quarterback publicly ridicules a player that has been benched.

### Snaps (What You'll Hear or See)

"You're worthless and you'll never achieve anything."
"I can't believe I wasted my time on someone like you."
"That dress makes you look fat—why did you wear it?"
"No one else would ever put up with your flaws."
"Your ideas are stupid; stick to what you're told."

### Penalty

Devaluation systematically chips away at self-esteem through criticism, insults, and humiliation, making the victim easier to control and less likely to resist.

### Role of the Offensive Unit (If Used)

Blockers follow the Quarterback's lead, ignoring or dismissing the benched player as no longer worthy of attention or respect.

### Challenge Flag

Eroding your sense of worth.

# Play #9 - Smear Campaign

### Football Play Name

Hurry-Up Offense (No Huddle)

### On-Field Analogy

The Quarterback calls rapid plays in succession, overwhelming the defense before it can reset. The speed and volume of the attack leave no time to respond or correct the record.

### Snaps (What You'll Hear or See)

"They have serious mental health issues and are unstable."
"I'm worried about them; they're constantly lying."
"They're the real abuser—I'm the victim."
"I had to leave because they were cheating."
"You shouldn't trust anything they say about me."

### Penalty

A smear campaign spreads lies, rumors, and half-truths to damage credibility and isolate the victim from support.

### Role of the Offensive Unit (If Used)

Blockers amplify and repeat the narrative, flooding the field with misinformation to confuse and overwhelm.

### Challenge Flag

Reputation destruction.

# Play #10 - Playing the Victim

## *Football Play Name*

Drawing the Roughing the Passer Foul

## *On-Field Analogy*

The Quarterback exaggerates false injury to draw a Penalty, shifting attention away from their behavior and onto the defender's supposed misconduct.

## *Snaps (What You'll Hear or See)*

"You're always attacking me; I'm just too sensitive."
"I do everything for you, and you hurt me."
"Look what you made me do."
"Everyone is against me."
"I'm fragile—you should know better."

## *Penalty*

Adopting victimhood to gain sympathy, avoid accountability, and redirect blame.

## *Role of the Offensive Unit (If Used)*

Blockers rush in to defend the QB, demanding punishment for the defender and reinforcing the false narrative.

## *Challenge Flag*

Weaponized victimhood.

# Play #11 - Future Faking

### Football Play Name

The Perpetual Goal Post Moving

### On-Field Analogy

The Quarterback promises a game-winning score but keeps moving the goal posts farther down the field, ensuring the victim never reaches them.

### Snaps (What You'll Hear or See)

"Once we move, everything will be better."
"I'll marry you next year."
"Just stick with me through this."
"We'll take that dream trip soon."
"I promise I'll change—just wait."

### Penalty

Using grand future promises to secure present compliance without intention of follow-through.

### Role of the Offensive Unit (If Used)

Blockers insist nothing has changed and the victim just needs to try harder.

### Challenge Flag

Hope used as leverage.

# Play #12 - Boundary Testing

### Football Play Name

Drawing the Defense Offsides

### On-Field Analogy

The Quarterback inches closer to the line again and again, testing how much movement will be tolerated before the defense reacts.

### Snaps (What You'll Hear or See)

"I know you said not to call late, but this is an emergency."
"I came over anyway—I missed you."
"It's not a big deal."
"I was just worried."
"You shouldn't keep secrets from me."

### Penalty

Repeatedly violating stated boundaries to erode safety and self-respect.

### Role of the Offensive Unit (If Used)

Blockers feign confusion about where the line even is, minimizing the violation.

### Challenge Flag

Testing what you'll allow.

# Play #13 - Word Salad

### Football Play Name
The Scramble Drill

### On-Field Analogy
The play collapses, and the Quarterback scrambles wildly, throwing short, meaningless passes to keep the play alive without advancing.

### Snaps (What You'll Hear or See)
"The issue is your tone"
"We're not talking about that."
"You're baiting me."
"That comparison makes no sense."
"You don't understand what I'm saying."

### Penalty
Overwhelming communication with confusion to derail accountability and resolution.

### Role of the Offensive Unit (If Used)
Blockers hold their positions, giving the QB time and space to keep talking.

### Challenge Flag
Disorientation through chaos.

# Play #14 - Baiting

### Football Play Name

The Trash Talk

### On-Field Analogy

The Quarterback taunts the defenders with the sole goal of provoking an emotional reaction that can then be penalized.

### Snaps (What You'll Hear or See)

"You're losing your mind."
"Why are you so angry?"
"If you yell, you're the problem."
"I'm just telling the truth."
"It's funny how worked up you get."

### Penalty

Deliberate provocation designed to trigger a reaction and shift blame.

### Role of the Offensive Unit (If Used)

Blockers watch closely, ready to point out the defender's reaction as proof they're unfit to play.

### Challenge Flag

Provoking reactions.

# Play #15 - Playing Dumb

### Football Play Name-

Delay of Game

### On-Field Analogy

The Quarterback pretends not to understand the rules or the last call to waste time while the clock runs down.

### Snaps (What You'll Hear or See)

"I have no idea what you're talking about—I don't remember any of that."

"That's too complicated for me; you handle it."

"Can you explain that again? I just don't get it—it's so confusing."

"You are so much better at handling money than I am."

"My mind is elsewhere; I can't focus on this right now."

### Penalty

Feigning ignorance or helplessness to avoid responsibility and shift effort onto the victim.

### Role of the Offensive Unit (If Used)

Blockers mirror the confusion, asking unnecessary questions to burn time and energy.

### Challenge Flag

Strategic incompetence.

# Play #16 - Isolation

## Football Play Name

The Zone Defense Breakdown

## On-Field Analogy

The Quarterback runs routes that pull key defenders out of position, leaving the victim alone and exposed in the middle of the field.

## Snaps (What You'll Hear or See)

"Your friends are a bad influence; they don't really like you."

"Your family doesn't truly understand our relationship."

"Why do you need to talk to anyone else when you have me?"

"I hate it when you spend time with them instead of me."

"I'm the only person in the world who truly understands you."

## Penalty

Systematically cutting off support systems to increase dependency.

## Role of the Offensive Unit (If Used)

Blockers intercept communication and discourage outside connection.

## Challenge Flag

Forced isolation.

# Play #17 - Intermittent Reinforcement

## Football Play Name

The "Free" Play

## On-Field Analogy

After repeated penalties, the Quarterback suddenly delivers a small positive gesture (a brief compliment, a minor apology) after a long series of penalties, ensuring the victim remains hopeful for a "fair game."

## Snaps (What You'll Hear or See)

(After a week of silent treatment) "You know I love you more than anything in the world."

(A thoughtful gift followed by a harsh criticism)

"You are the best at this, but you are still a complete mess."

"We had such a good night—why did you have to ruin it by saying that?"

"I'll be nice to you if you stop doing the things that annoy me."

## Penalty

Mixing kindness and harm to create emotional addiction (trauma bonding).

## Role of the Offensive Unit (If Used)

Blockers highlight this singular, small positive action as proof that the Quarterback is a good sport, making the victim overlook the 99 terrible plays that came before it.

## Challenge Flag

Inconsistent reinforcement.

# Play #18 - Minimization

### Football Play Name

The Finger Point after Fumble

### On-Field Analogy

The Quarterback insists that nothing significant happened and that they still have the ball, pointing as though this is true, despite clear evidence on the field.

### Snaps (What You'll Hear or See)

"It was just a joke—why are you so sensitive?"
"You're blowing this completely out of proportion."
"I barely even touched you, stop being dramatic."
"Other people have it much worse than you do."
"Get over it, it was a minor incident."

### Penalty

Downplaying harm to invalidate the victim's experience.

### Role of the Offensive Unit (If Used)

Blockers blindly follow the Quarterback's insistence that they have the ball and inaccurately start pointing.

### Challenge Flag

Downplaying the impact of their actions.

# Play #19 - Shaming

### Football Play Name

Illegal Block in the Back

### On-Field Analogy

A hit or push from behind that pushes or shoves the opponent unsuspectingly.

### Snaps (What You'll Hear or See)

"Only a truly terrible person would think or do that."
"You should be ashamed of yourself for being so selfish."
"Everyone knows what a disaster you are."
"You are a disgrace to your family or profession."
"How can you live with yourself after that mistake?"

### Penalty

Attacking core identity to induce guilt and humiliation.

### Role of the Offensive Unit (If Used)

Blockers justify the hit, blaming the victim for being too weak or sensitive.

### Challenge Flag

Attacking core self-worth.

# Play #20 - Entitlement

### Football Play Name

Arguing with the Referee

### On-Field Analogy

The Quarterback demands yardage without running a play, insisting the rules don't apply to them.

### Snaps (What You'll Hear or See)

"Do you know who I am? I shouldn't have to wait."
"The rules don't apply to people like me."
"I deserve to have the best, regardless of the cost."
"You owe me this, it's my right."
"That is beneath my attention."

### Penalty

Demanding special treatment and exemption from accountability.

### Role of the Offensive Unit (If Used)

Blockers argue the Quarterback is too important/special to be questioned.

### Challenge Flag

Rule exemption.

# Play #21 - Rage/Explosive Anger

## Football Play Name

Panic Throw

## On-Field Analogy

Facing a potential sack, the Quarterback makes a reckless, dangerous throw that terrifies everyone on the field.

## Snaps (What You'll Hear or See)

(Screaming at the top of their lungs over a minor mistake)
"Don't you ever challenge me again!"
"If you keep pushing me, you'll regret it."
(Breaking an object to show their level of anger)
"I'll make your life a living hell if you disobey me."

## Penalty

Using fear and intimidation to silence opposition. If this play is present, safety—not understanding—becomes the priority.

## Role of the Offensive Unit (If Used)

Blockers blame the victim for being "in the way" rather than the Quarterback for making the reckless move.

## Challenge Flag

Fear-based control.

# Play #22 - Emotional Blackmail

### Football Play Name

The Hail Mary Interception Threat

### On-Field Analogy

The Quarterback poorly executes a hail Mary pass that will result in an interception.

### Snaps (What You'll Hear or See)

"If you leave me, I'll hurt myself, and it will be your fault."

"A good partner would never deny me this request."

"I'll tell everyone your secret if you don't comply."

"If you truly loved me, you would do this for me."

"You owe me after everything I've done for you."

### Penalty

Using guilt, fear, or threat to force compliance.

### Role of the Offensive Unit (If Used)

Blockers insist the victim is responsible for preventing disaster and saving the game.

### Challenge Flag

Coerced obedience.

# Play #23 - Warping Time

### Football Play Name

The Clock Management Foul

### On-Field Analogy

The Quarterback manipulates the game clock—stretching painful moments and shrinking positive ones—to control the narrative.

### Snaps (What You'll Hear or See)

"I didn't say that yesterday, I said it a month ago, and it was a joke."
"That event happened completely differently and lasted only five minutes."
"You're holding onto something that happened years ago, get over it."
"It feels like forever since you paid attention to me."
"You were the one who started that argument last week, not me."

### Penalty

Distorting timelines to invalidate memory and reality.

### Role of the Offensive Unit (If Used)

Blockers insist the clock is fine and the victim is impatient.

### Challenge Flag

Manipulating the chronology of events.

# Play #24 - Grandiosity

### Football Play Name

Unsportsmanlike Conduct

### On-Field Analogy

The Quarterback celebrates as if they've already won, ignoring the impact on everyone else.

### Snaps (What You'll Hear or See)

(A cold, blank stare when you express deep sadness)
"Why are you crying? Stop being a baby, it's not a big deal."
"I don't care about your problems, I have my own things to deal with."
"Your pain is your problem, not mine."
"Focus on my needs for once, not your little issues."

### Penalty

Inability to recognize or care about others' feelings.

### Role of the Offensive Unit (If Used)

Blockers cheer wildly and carry the Quarterback on their shoulders, reinforcing the delusion of superiority and entitlement.

### Challenge Flag

Emotional abandonment.

# Conclusion

This playbook has walked you through the most common narcissistic plays—how they're run, what they sound like, who helps carry them out, and the cost to your health and well-being. If nothing else, understanding these patterns affirms a critical truth: what you experienced was real.

Awareness and validation are powerful, but they are not the end of the game. Once you can recognize the plays, read the snaps, and see the Blockers in motion, the question becomes what happens next. Defense is not about confrontation or winning arguments—it's about protecting your energy, reclaiming your clarity, and choosing where you engage.

The next step is learning how to counter the plays without sacrificing yourself in the process. *The Invincible Defense: Counter to the Narcissist's Playbook* offers real-world examples and practical strategies for building a defense that holds—one grounded in boundaries, discernment, and self-trust. The offense may keep calling the same plays, but once you see the field clearly, you don't have to stay in the game.

# About the Author

Dr. Tina Paone is a licensed professional counselor, registered play therapist–supervisor, counselor educator, and tenured professor with more than 25 years of experience in the mental health field. Throughout her career, she has trained future therapists, led social justice initiatives, and supported survivors of complex trauma in reclaiming their lives.

Dr. Paone brings a rare dual lens to her work: deep clinical expertise paired with lived experience. In her forthcoming memoir, *UNBROKEN: Healing from Narcissistic Abuse and Reclaiming Me* (May 2026), she writes with clarity, authority, and compassion about surviving childhood grooming, emotional neglect, a coercive marriage, and post-separation abuse. The book is more than her story—it is a mirror for those still finding their voice.

Her current clinical focus centers on supporting survivors of narcissistic abuse and trauma-entrenched family systems. She is also a sought-after speaker and workshop facilitator whose work spans therapy, education, and advocacy.

She is also, fittingly, a lifelong Philadelphia Eagles fan, which means she believes in resilience, knows how to survive painful seasons, and never stops showing up, even when the game gets brutal.

Learn more about Dr. Paone's work—and subscribe to her newsletter—at drtinapaone.com.

www.ingramcontent.com/pod-product-compliance
Lightning Source LLC
Chambersburg PA
CBHW071226130626
46555CB00004B/1860